Poetry
of
a
Man's Soul

By William Arnold

All rights reserved.
Copyright 2020 ©
ISBN: 978-1-7343610-6-3
Second Printed Edition

All rights reserved under International Copyright Law. No part of this book may be stored or reproduced in any form without the express written permission of the author. Permission requests must be directed and approved in writing by author.
Printed in the United States

PlayPen Publishing
Ellenwood, GA

This book of poetry is dedicated to my family, mother, father, sisters, brothers, and children.

Table of Contents

Acknowledgement 8
What I Am 10
Child Guidance And Parenting 12
To Love One Another 14
Love That Drink 16
Survival 18
Who Are Our Kids' Heroes 20
Christmas Bypass My Door 22
I Wish It Would Cry 24
A Man's Daily Prayer For His Family 26
When You're Away 28
A Line Can Be Straight 30
If The World Was A Football Team 32
Looking Into A Mirror 34
Family Values 36
Tomorrow Today And Yesterday 38
To Teach A Child 40
I'm Too Fat 42
Words Of A Man 44
What They're Trying To Say 46
What's Your Religion 48
A Day To Be Thankful 50
When There's No Bottom To Run To 52

~ Poetry of a Man's Soul ~

Table of Contents

The Soul Of A Man 54
To Be A Man 56
Welfare 58
Does Love Have Color 60
Stepfather 62
What My Dad Means To Me 64
Mr. Afro-American Man 66
The Mind And Worlds Of A Child 68
Where My Heart Is 70
What's The Matter With This World 72
My Child Was Born Today 74
What Am I Going To Do This Summer 76
Hunger 78
Who Shall We Love 80
American Cowboy Who Is He 82
To Hate 84
Divorce 86
Why Am I So Lucky 88
Why Do I Love You 90
To Be Ready To Go 92
When You're Born Poor 94
Your 50th Birthday 96
Final Thoughts 98

~ Poetry of a Man's Soul ~

~ Poetry of a Man's Soul ~

What's More Important
Than A Man's Soul?
What Is That?
A Man Can Have
All The Riches
In The World
And Lose His Soul!

~ Poetry of a Man's Soul ~

A Note To The Reader

In *Poetry of A Man's Soul,* every poem is accompanied by a paragraph for you, the reader, to try and understand what the writer is trying to express to you.

~ Poetry of a Man's Soul ~

What I Am was my first poem. It was about me as a person and the things around me. People have called me all kinds of names but no one told me who I was. I don't care about the color of my skin because no one can change that. What is in my heart is what I care about. I just want all men to know "What I Am". I am an American. I was born here and there is nothing you can do to me to change that. Until the day I die, I am a man born free in AMERICA!

What I Am

To be a Man I've been called all colors
Some say I am a Colored Man, some say I am a Negro
Some say I am Black and some say I'm African-American
But they all forget to call me What I Am
For my skin may be dark and some of our skin may be light
Some say I'm crazy and some say I'm lazy
Some say I'm a thief in the dark
But no one says What I Am
Some say I have a mind but a small mind to think
Some say I'm a Red Man mixed with White
But What I Am
All said, I have the blood of them all but let me say
That you are so blind to really not see What I Am
First, A Man that lives in a land where all Men are said to be free
For Black, White, Yellow, or Red ... What I Am
You all need to know first, I am a Man of Color
But out of all these things that I like to be
So every Man, Woman and Child can see
That What I Am is an American BORN FREE
I am an American and God Bless Thee
The words of a Man that is surely FREE

~ Poetry of a Man's Soul ~

Child Guidance And Parenting When I wrote this passage, I hoped when you read it you would understand about us and our children. What they really need is love from me and you as parents. Our kids will have so many problems in the world. So love and understanding must start at home. LOVE OUR CHILDREN and they will love you.

Child Guidance And Parents

Everybody is looking for the right book or advice that will tell them what the problem is with their child. You read the newspapers and books, watch talk shows, listen to the radio and even look to the government in order to tell you about your child. Everybody is looking for the right idea explaining your child's behavior. You don't have to look anymore. If you would just take a couple of minutes to go to your bedroom, bathroom, or living room, there is something there that can help you. When you find it, look at it very hard because that may be your child's worse problem. It is a mirror. Look into it and see where your child's problems start. Some parents are just like an alcoholic who will not acknowledge the problem until it is too late. All of this centers around the way you give your child guidance. For a child is born into this world with one thing and only one thing. He or she is looking for us as parents to love, take care of them and instill family values. Our children don't ask for single parents. They deserve to know who is Mother and who is Father. They don't deserve to have a world filled with divorce, child abuse, drugs and hate. They didn't come into this world looking for all of these problems. Sometimes it's like our kids are born into a jungle and they are on their own! We don't have time for them; we work all the time, come home tired, and leave them to deal with their own problems. You must understand! No matter how bad you think a child is, remember; he or she is only a child. So stop to understand what is happening to our children. We must go back to the basics and back to family values. People want to know that there is hope for their children. Maybe the question should be, "Is there hope for us?"

~ Poetry of a Man's Soul ~

To Love One Another We as Americans should love one another above all things. Our future and past were built on love and that's the way it should be. We must understand if we the people must live together, first, we must learn to love one another. So this poem is for those who don't understand the love of all mankind.

To Love One Another

We work together, White, Black, Yellow, or Red
We fight together in wars, side by side; we even died together
In countries far away, we make men free
But when we leave our jobs, we walk alone
Black with Black, Red with Red, Yellow with Yellow and
White with White
We can't even go to church together
But, aren't we all Americans living in the Land of the Free?
This is not the time for you to hate me
I bleed, you bleed, I die, you die;you lie and so do I
But when we talk about just coming over for dinner,
It's as if we had started a war
Black men, White men, Red men and Yellow
It's time for us all to live TOGETHER
When you see me in the store
You walk by me as if you never saw me before
When you invite your friends over for a party, you don't invite me?
Is it because of my color?
We are all Americans. I don't care what you say
It's time for you and me to live together
Why do people hate you because of your color?
It's not the time to hate. It's the time to love one another
If I took your baby and my baby and put them in the same playpen,
They would play together and be friends
So the hate is not born within, it was put in
So why not live together and love one another?

~ Poetry of a Man's Soul ~

Love That Drink It's the love of alcohol and what it does to a man's family and friends. How can drinking change your whole life around with just one dose? Why do we as people feel we must have this drink called ALCOHOL? It has made people lose their jobs, wind up in jail and most of all, loss their family and friends.

Love That Drink

When you drink, you're an alcoholic?
Does it make you big and tall?
Does it make you the man that you want to be?
What does it do to a man like you and me?
Does it make that man come out that you understand?
Is this the man you always wanted to be?
Then why do we take it out on the one's that we love?
What is this that makes us fight, kill and die?
With just one dose?
Is it a drug or is it a disease?
Why does it take us and makes a monkey out of us?
When you drink, does it make you weak?
Tell me, if that's the case, then what do we need it for?
Tell me, tell me, are we all insane?
Why do we love that drink called ALCOHOL?

~ Poetry of a Man's Soul ~

Survival, is a poem about life. People say that they don't understand why they are killing, stealing, robbing, and abusing drugs. Today just like in the early years after the Civil War, people were free and still didn't have a job. They started to do the same as our kids are doing today and that's "SURVIVAL". When there are no jobs and no one around who cares, there's no one to teach them right from wrong. If you catch an animal in a trap, it will chew off its' leg for its' "SURVIVAL". That's what some of the kids of today are doing. It's the best they know how and that's called "SURVIVAL" to you and me.

SURVIVAL

To take a man and lock him in jail
Are you trying to give him hell?
When you take him and put him in a pen
Are you trying to make him think of his sin?
We build jails and build more
Is that stopping crime? I'd like to know!
I went to the jail
There I saw young man after young man in and out the door
I asked and asked, "Why are you here?"
They said because they had nothing to do
"I'm not working for $4.50 an hour
When I can rob you for your dollar."
"Why not go to school and get a better education, " I asked.
"To finish high school is a joke," they said.
To come out and hear the man holler
 "I don't have the experience to make this dollar."
Where do I run to? Tell me sir
Where are the people that do care?
Our leaders are bought and paid for every day
Tell me, tell me, You think they care?
As we run the streets, it's a jungle out there
It takes money to live today
So, I'm going to rob and steal every way
What is your future?
You will say I don't know today
But if you think I live to die, you're wrong
No, I live to survive
No matter how

~ Poetry of a Man's Soul ~

Who Are Our Kids' Heroes, is a poem for all men to read. Our kids' "HERO" needs to be YOU! Our kids don't need to look up to anyone but you, their HERO. Let our kids look up to us as a role model. Don't let them turn to someone on TV or some guy that plays sports. Let that love and admiration shine upon you.

Who Are Our Kids' Heroes?

Who are the heroes that our kids need to look up to?
Are they the guys that run up and down the basketball court?
Or, baseball or football field tall and true?
Is it the Lawyer and Cowboy that they need to look up to?
Do you know who are our kids' heroes?
Their heroes are you and me
For our kids need only one thing in life and that is
Love and Understanding and Guidance from you and me
That Father's love that is so true
They can grow up to be heroes too
A hero is a man of distinguish value
The person who has the principal share in some exploits
He works hard
What better hero than Dad is there?
Our kids' hero is not a basketball player playing on the court
Or a baseball or football player playing on the field
Most of them need help too
Our kids' hero must start at home
It's you Dad!
Our hero through and through must be YOU!

~ Poetry of a Man's Soul ~

Christmas Bypass My House, is a poem about the kids who miss Christmas every year. We are people giving too much to children that don't need it. Sometimes we forget about the kids that are truly in need. If you only knew what it was like for them during the holidays. They don't get any toys and that should bring a tear to your eye. All kids want is the feeling of being just like everyone else. It's not their fault that poverty has a hold of their household.

Christmas Bypass My Door

I looked out the window
I heard a child say "Christmas is near!"
As I ran down to the store to buy the kids some toys,
I remembered the year when Christmas passed my door
Only toy I had that year was a little rock I found on the floor
My father had lost his job that year
Everything was so hard for us
But it's America, Land of the Free
It shouldn't be hard for a kid like me
I knew with all my heart that Christmas would bypass my door
As I watched Santa Clause in every store
I knew there was no way he would come pass my door
I heard my father say, "I'm sorry son.
We don't have any money this year to buy a toy."
"But, Santa Clause will come Dad.
I know he will bring me a toy on Christmas day!"
I sat up half the night trying to wait on Santa Clause
Then I fell asleep
I woke up and to my surprise
Christmas did bypass my door this year
It made a little man out of me
A tear came out my eye but I said, "I'm not going to cry!
I'm going to stand tall this year and just thank God for being here."
The year Christmas bypassed my door

~ Poetry of a Man's Soul ~

I Wish It Would Cry, is a poem about the love of a parent for their kid. In a world where there is more hate than understanding, our kids need someone to look up to. Parents can see all of the world's hate. Yet, children see the world through rose-colored glasses. That is until it's too late and that child is loss to the world and all of it's temptations.

I Wish It Would Cry

Why does a baby cry?
It cries to tell you, "I need to be fed. Will you come feed me please?"
It cries because sometimes it feels you're so sad
It cries because it wants you to hold it tight and
Tell it that you love it with all of your might
It cries to make you hold it so that you can think
The world is his and yours when that baby is in your arms
Eventually that baby gets older and stops crying
Then, it begins to talk
To tell you...
"Mom can I have some money to get something to eat?"
"Mom, I need some money for clothes."
Then when you hug them they will say...
"Mom, I'm too old for that today."
You'll try to tell your kid you care and will love them in every way.
Do you try to do the small things that you used to?
That kid may turn it's back and walk away
You know there will be problems and a Mom can see
All the hate the world will have for thee
Tears in your eyes and you will say
"I just wish time could go back and my baby would cry today!"

~ Poetry of a Man's Soul ~

A Man's Daily Prayer, is a poem for all Men that believe in GOD! Thank GOD for every day that your family has never seen before. Together, a family should give thanks for every blessing.

A Man's Daily Prayer For His Family

Thank you God for waking me and my family up this morning
To give us a day that we have never seen before
While we were sleeping, you blessed us to wake once more
You blessed us with our health and strength this morning
To walk today in your way
So dear Lord with all our hearts, we'd like to say
"Thank you for this day."
For many have not been as blessed to see this day
We can't tell you how important it is
Thank you again for this day
We can't tell you how important it is
To give my family and me the strength and the way
To keep on serving you every day

-Amen
A Man's Daily Prayer... every day

~ Poetry of a Man's Soul ~

When You're Away, is a poem about the love that a man should have for his woman. He should tell her how much he cares. Sometimes men forget to say the small words that mean so much to the ones he loves. **When You're Away** is a love letter from the author to all his love ones and maybe someone will read this and feel the same way.

When You're Away

When I walk around the house, it's sad but true
A house is not a home without you
It seems even the flowers are prettier when you're around
The years that we have been together sing a sound
You are my heaven My angel true
When you're not here, everything is blue
When you're not home with me and on the go
Time passes so very slow
They say a man's home is his castle supreme
But what is a castle without a queen
All my life is based around loving you
At day's end, I want to just take care of you
I go to sleep with you on my mind
Dreaming of the woman I was lucky to find
If there is a heaven and you're not there
It would be so sad and completely unfair
So, with all of my heart, I'd like to say
Darling a house is not a home when you're away!

~ Poetry of a Man's Soul ~

A Line Can Be Straight, is a poem about people's love. Is it really love? Is it a game that people play? Look and see what love has done to you and your friends. People will tell you a lie before they tell you the truth when it comes to love.

A Line Can Be Straight

A line can be straight and so can a street
When someone gives their heart, why aren't they?
Can a line from your mouth hurt you more?
Are you straight when you tell me that you love me so?
But is it only a line that's not straight anymore
Why do people give you a line to tell you they care?
A line can be straight and so can a street
But why can't people be straight with their feelings?
Honesty is a MUST!

~ Poetry of a Man's Soul ~

If The World Was A Football Team, is a poem about the love for our brothers and sisters. Whatever the color, love one another.

If The World Was A Football Team

If the World was a Football Team
And all the people were players
Wasn't it nice, when we did things right?
We would all hug each other
We would play as a team
We would eat, sleep and work together
Most of all, we would love one another
Couch would tell us what to do
"Work as a team! Win as a team!"
"When we lose, we lose as a team!"
When things go wrong, the team is there
To give you a helping hand
We keep playing until we are all winners
We play to find ourselves and understand how good we are
We learn that whatever you are, you are team mates
Most important, the players are your friends
When we fight, we fight as a team and not against one another!
The only color we see is our team color
When the game is over, we leave the field as losers or winners
Those are our friends on the winning team
Within our heart, we love and support each other until the END!

~ Poetry of a Man's Soul ~

Looking Into A Mirror, is a poem about what a Mother or Father should be. When a child looks at you to see guidance. It's more of a reflection of what a parent should be.

Looking Into A Mirror

When you look into a mirror who do you see?
Is it a reflection of you or how you really see?
Do you know that person, or is it someone else?
A mirror can only see what's there, but is it really you?
When your kids look at you, who do they see?
Is it only Father?
What should a Father be like when they look at you?
What do they see?
Is it a reflection of what a Father should be?
Who are you and the things that you see?
When only a mirror is looking at you, can it really tell the truth?
People, a mirror can only show a reflection of you
Who sees the real you?
Can it see that you're happy?
Can it see that you are so sad?
Can it see when someone has made you mad?
What does a mirror see when it looks at you?
When life is all up and down
Is it the mirror that you turn to when no one is around?
So what does a MIRROR see that I don't see in you?
What the mirror sees is the real YOU!

~ Poetry of a Man's Soul ~

Family Values, is a poem about one of the most important things that all people need. We must understand that without the family love, we as a people can't and won't make it. We as parents can say that it takes only one parent to be a family and raise a child but a family is more than that. We don't know what a family is. When will we, the people, learn that what America is made of is family, love, and understanding.

Family Values

When you walk out that door every morning to go to work
Walk back into the house
Look at what you're going to work for
It's the family that you support
The little ones, as they run through the house
Telling you, Dad, how much they care
Because without you, the whole family has fallen
It takes two to keep a family going
It's Mom and Dad.
I don't care what anyone says
It must take two to care
Mom is there with all the love and she helps keep things going
It's YOU Dad that stands strong and tells me when I'm wrong
A family is just what it says
A FAMILY is three or more
Dad is the head and Mom is the foundation
The kids are the future standing tall
This is how a family will make it
Whenever things go wrong
This is the "Family Value" that will keep them strong!

~ Poetry of a Man's Soul ~

Today, Tomorrow and Yesterday, is a poem about men that forget to tell their loved ones how much they mean. Tomorrow is promised to no one. Speak the words of your heart while you can and ensure there are no regrets.

Tomorrow, Today and Yesterday

Yesterday is gone and Tomorrow is promised to no one
Today, I like to say all the ways I love you
Sometimes we forget to tell the words that are so dear to you
Sometimes men forget to say the words that you like to hear
So darling, I would like to say the words that are so dear to me
I love thee
I love you for yesterday that's gone and I can't bring back
All the times I forget to tell how much I care
All the things that you do for me without me
I want to show you how much I care
I know that yesterday is gone
Tomorrow is promised to no one
So today with all my heart, I would like to say darling,
I LOVE YOU

~ Poetry of a Man's Soul ~

To Teach A Child, is a poem about you as a teacher of your child. To teach a child, we must know how to teach our children to care. Why is it today that we must read books about how to fix a child's behavior? How is it that we, this new generation with great minds, know nothing about how to be a parent and how to teach your children?

To Teach A Child

How do you teach your child?
We tell our kids right from wrong
We tell them not to drink alcohol
Then, every Friday and Saturday night,
We are sitting in the front of the TV with a 6 pack
We tell our kids not to use bad language
Then, when you get mad, every other word is a cuss word
We tell our kids not to do drugs
Then, they see you in the kitchen with a blunt
You tell your kids not to fight
Then, every Friday and Saturday, you get drunk and fight all night
You tell your kids that sex is wrong at an early age
But you know that you were a wild child!
A kid is a kid
He or she learns by what they see from you and me
You tell your kids that it's wrong to smoke cigarettes
It's bad for their breath
Every time they see you, you look like a smoke stack
The little things that you do around them will change their whole life around
So when you see them with a pack of cigarettes and a beer is missing from the refrigerator, you know they are copying you!
They're fighting in school and struggling to learn.
Being teen parents is like kids raising kids
Ask yourself do I know how to teach my child when I can't teach myself?

~ Poetry of a Man's Soul ~

I'm Too Fat, is a poem for people that talk about you're size. When God made man, he made us all sizes and all to look different. So why are you trying to tell me what size I should be? I know you're saying it's for my health. Or, is it for your pocketbook? If you don't like me for my size, you just don't have to look at me. People must understand to let people be themselves and leave them alone

I'm Too Fat

They said that I'm too fat I need to be on a diet
They said if I don't lose weight, I'm going to die
As I was walking one day, I was thinking about what people had said
When along came a man jogging so he could to lose weight
He got hit by a truck!
The last I heard, he was a whole lot smaller
As I walked past a fitness center, I was looking and saw women passed out on the floor
I went to the store to buy some clothes there was a woman in there holding a size 8
She was saying it was too large
She said she has to get down to a size 4
All these people, so sad but true
They don't know what to do
So I made up my mind, if you don't like my size
Let me tell you what to do
I'm fat, I'm happy, and always with a smile
I eat what I want
I drink what I want and sleep good at night
So don't get on me if you're sad and blue
If God wanted me small, he would have made me small
Look at me because I know what size I am
I am not sad and blue, when I look at you.
I don't have a problem
The problem is you
Look at yourself always sad and blue.
I don't tell you what to eat or what to do
Oh yes, by the way, have you ever heard of a fat person attacking or hurting you?

~ Poetry of a Man's Soul ~

Words Of A Man, is a poem about being a man. No man should have to be a certain COLOR in order to get a job. When I apply for a job, look at me as a man and that's all!

Words Of A MAN

When I apply for a job,
Don't put a title over my head and call me a M I N OR I T Y
Put that title on me that I can understand
Call me a M A N
I don't want you to give me a job because the government tells you too
Give me a job because you know that I am the qualified MAN
I'm not looking for a handout to be a MAN
I'm just looking for a job
Don't make me a token to just have around
I'm looking for a future in my job
All I want to be is an AMERICAN
A man born free
I have the freedom to vote, to live, and raise my family
I want my kids to go to school and get a better education
I want my kids to be people to look up to
Don't put a title over my head and tell me
THE ONLY WAY I CAN GET THIS JOB IS TO BE A MINORITY
I am a man
I put on my pants just like you
I bleed and cry just like you
I'm sorry if my color is a problem to you
I'm here to stay and teach everyone to love one another.
So if you have a job for me, please give it to me
Don't just look at my color because I am more than my color
I am MAN!

~ Poetry of a Man's Soul ~

What They're Trying To Say, is a poem about me or you when our kids are telling us things and we can't connect. It's the things around us that we must understand in order to find out what they're trying to say.

Words Of A MAN

When your walking into church every Sunday and
You have something new on
What are you trying to do?
Get someone's attention?
When you buy that fine new car and nice home
What are trying to do?
Get someone's attention?
When you go to work and
Your boss tells you that you have a promotion
What do you do?
Do you try and get some attention?
When things go on around you, why can't you see?
Is someone trying to get your attention?
When their grades are falling from A's to D's,
What are they trying to say?
When he stays out at night until 2
Tell me what they're saying to you
When your money is missing from your pocket book
Tell me, tell me, what are they trying to say?
When you try to hold them and they walk away
Are they trying to say something to you?
Is it too late or do you understand what they're trying to do?
It's just like the nose on your face

~ Poetry of a Man's Soul ~

What's Your Religion, is a poem about you and what you believe in. Some people say that they have no religion, but this poem is trying to ask you to find your own religion. In this day and time, we all need a faith to live by.

What's Your Religion

They said that religion is an acknowledgement
Or is it our obligation to GOD?
What is your religion?
What do you believe in?
Is it God?
To believe in GOD, is it all you need to know?
For with GOD, man can find all hope
We all know right from wrong and how to love one another
So where do you find your religion?
Is it only in the church that you go to?
Your religion should be in your heart
You love GOD and all mankind
How can you love something that you've never seen?
How can you hate your neighbor that lives next door?
There are all kinds of religion
Have you ever wondered why?
Some people can serve their GOD and do what they want to do
Do they think they can go to heaven too.
Things that you know are wrong, but you just have to have it
It says in the BIBLE that JESUS drank wine
But it doesn't say that he had to have a bottle every day
Religion is a man's HEART and SOUL and he must believe in God
Religion is a 7 day a week and 24 hour job
It's not Sunday to the next Sunday when you meet in church
Because one Sunday you might not make it back
So what is religion?
It's a 24 hour and a 7 day a week job in serving GOD

~ Poetry of a Man's Soul ~

A Day To Be Thankful, is a poem about a day for all men to look forward to because today is a day that God has given to you. Even if you're sick or down to the ground, THANK GOD for being here.

A Day To Be Thankful

As I walked outside today
I thanked GOD for a pretty day
But someone said, "How can it be pretty when it's raining today?"
I told them that if it rains, today, tomorrow, and the next day too
It's a day you have never seen before
So thank GOD for being here
It's a day that GOD has blessed the WORLD wit
You are blessed to be here.
That's why I said, "No matter what the weather is today,
GOD have given you a new."
It's a day to be thankful for!

~ Poetry of a Man's Soul ~

There's No Bottom To Run To, is a poem about when we as people, killed us all. Who will be there to hold your hand when you have killed us all?

There's No Bottom To Run To

Where does a man go when there ain't no bottom below?
It's sad but true
Where do you run to when the man has taken the bottom from you?
You have never been on the top, and now you lost your bottom too
They're getting you so you're killing your brothers
Robbing your mother and raping your sister too
Tell me, tell me, that's not true
What in the hell shall we do?
It's time to look at yourself and see how you are
When you are so far to the ground, there is no where to run to
Killing, Murder, Theft and Drugs too
When there's no one around, but only you
There's no bottom for you to run to
It's got to be you and me to stand tall
But, you're going to kill us all
They kill the head and they got you killing the body
Then, there will be no bottom to run to
Look my brother and live so we all can live
If you don't change, there will be no bottom to run to!

~ Poetry of a Man's Soul ~

The Soul Of A Man, is a poem about a man who looks into his soul. If we did this, it would help us all. When a man loses his soul, where does he go? It is hell below. With all the hell on earth, why should we as men lose our souls? We need love and understanding to help our SOUL.

The Soul Of A Man

What are you?
Are you just Flesh and blood?
Are you a man with a soul?
They say when you die, you are just a body
But when you're living, are you just flesh and blood?
Are you a man with a soul?
What do I see when I look at you?
Am I looking at your soul
Or just flesh and blood?
When you leave this old world, does your soul go one way
And your bones left in the ground?
When you do the things of this world, are you in this world?
Is it your soul, when you do the things that you do?
How can a man's soul let you do what you do to mankind?
What happens to a man when his soul is gone?
When the spiritual principle in a man has gone
When his moral and emotional part is gone
When the nature elevation of his mind is gone
What happens?
Tell me, tell me, where is your soul?
How can you do this to mankind?
Killing, Raping, and Murdering?
Where is your soul?
Did it leave you and will it come back?
Will it come back after you did what you have done?
A man's soul is all he has
When he loses his soul, he has lost all hope
Where do you go when you lose your soul?
Your only direction is hell below

~ Poetry of a Man's Soul ~

To Be A Man, is a poem about what it means to be a man. It's about learning what it takes to be a man, to be a Father, to raise a family, to be strong, learning right from wrong, learning to do things that everyone can look up to. I hope you will understand what I'm trying to say to you. A man has the future for all mankind within his hands.

To Be A Man

To be a man is so hard to do for a young child like yo.
A Man is a human being, a male adult
A boy is a male child trying to be a young MAN
A teenager is a young man trying to be a MAN
In the early stages of manhood, you have a chance to be a man
When you take that away, what do you have?
A boy needs to be a boy
He needs to be allowed to grow up and do the things that boys do
A boy cannot be a man until he experiences being a boy
To play, to cry, to laugh, and to have fun are important
But, the most important thing is that he is loved by us
Then after that, he can be a teenager or a young man
To drive his father's car for the very first time
To have his first date
To be a leader on his team
To say yes sir, no sir, and understand right from wrong
To understand what he was put here for
To grow up
To be a man and raise his family
He will understand that job of being a MAN
His kids will see what it takes to be a MAN
With that we all can be strong and raise our families to be big and tall

~ Poetry of a Man's Soul ~

Welfare, is a poem about one thing and it must be stopped. Welfare is only a crutch for all mankind. For today and the next, we must stop it. We must want to help ourselves and not help ourselves to a handout.

Welfare

As you ride past the ghetto, do you feel sad and blue?
To see how those people live, it couldn't be true
They are living so bad and don't know what to do
Man you better wake up and think because
They're living better than you
Every morning I go to hear the Man say "Hey BOY!
Why are you late today?"
Then he's on your back everyday
He's trying to make you walk away
Then if that's not bad, but true
Miss two pay days and you're through
1/3 of your pay check goes to pay your rent
1/3 goes to buy something to eat
And the last 1/3 is for taxes which pays for THEIR rent
This is so sad but true
I hear a teenage girl say she's going to live off WELFARE,
Off me and you
I went down to the corner store to buy me something to eat
In front of me was a woman wearing a mink coat
She stood there holding food stamps
Her Cadillac was outside and parked close to the store
I looked at my wife and she looked back at me
You keep on bringing that small pay check home
And I'll be on it too
I got a letter from the IRS and they said
If you don't pay your taxes BOY you are through
Oh man! What am I going to do?
Are you trying tear me down?
Are you trying to put my family on the WELFARE LINE?
Are you trying to put my family back in slavery?
Chained to the ground?

~ Poetry of a Man's Soul ~

Does Love Have Color, is a poem about why in America where all men are said to be free, I should only love one color? If a man's heart is true, then love has no color

Does Love Have Color

When I saw her it was love at first sight
When she saw me it was the same
I looked at her and asked her for her hand
That was all I took
I told my mother I had fallen in love and she said it was great
THEN, I told her who she was and she said,
"Out of all the women in this WORLD
You had to fall in love with THAT girl?"
She told her father that she was in love
And then she told him who I was and he said,
"Out of all the men in this WORLD
You had to fall in love with THAT man?"
When people look at us as we walk the streets
They turn and look at us as if we were wrong
If it is wrong to fall in love with someone other than your color?
Should black be with black, white with white, red with red,
And yellow with yellow?
Is that the way it should be, tell me, tell me?
What should we do?
This is AMERICAN, land of the free
All men are the same, you and me
Why is it wrong to be in love with someone of another color
From 10 long years from that day
We have learned to love one another in every way
If it's so wrong, I'm happy to say
No matter what...
We are going to be in love EVERY DAY

~ Poetry of a Man's Soul ~

Stepfather is a poem about a man that fell in love with a woman with kids. I look at this with all my heart and say to myself, it's very hard for what I'm trying to do. It's more downs than ups but I tried. When a man does this, know you are not only taking on a wife and kids. You are taking on the baggage from all past relationships.

Stepfather

Stepfather, how am I?
The man that fell in love with a woman one day
Just because she had three kids, he could walk away
I tried with all my heart to make a way
I tried to make them love me in every way
I tried to give her and the kids things they never had
But not being their father is hard some days
The kids see me as only their stepfather
God knows in my heart I tried to love them in every way
I tried to give them a whole family
But I guess they just don't want me around
Did they just want things their way?
To be a stepfather is hard in every way
I heard the kids say one day
I hope he moves away because we don't need a stepfather
TODAY

~ Poetry of a Man's Soul ~

What My Dad Means To Me, is a poem written by my daughter Tiffany Arnold-June 7, 1988.

What My Dad Means to Me

My DAD means a lot to me.
He takes me to the swimming pool and Showbib Pizza.
My DAD is sweet, the kindest man in the World,
But one thing my MOM and DAD are not together.
My dad is the MAN I love forever and ever.
Last night I went to his house and spent the night
And my dog was there.
When it got dark, my dad and I went to sleep.
Then I got up the next day, me and my dad went to Six Flags.
We always have a good time when we're together.
My DAD is sweet and he is getting sweeter every day.
If my DAD would let me have one wish,
I wish him and mother were together today.
OOPS... I forgot something.
I love you, my DAD.

~ Poetry of a Man's Soul ~

Why? Why? **_Mr. Afro-American Man,_** let's live together and love one another.

Mr. Afro-American Man

I want to know as an Afro-American man
Why do we think we need a drink of alcohol in our hand to be a man?
Why do we need a cigarette or a gun in our hand?
Mr. Afro-American man
Do we respect our women and our children?
Do we respect our fellow man?
Tell me, tell me, Mr. Afro-American man
Do we need to sell drugs to be an Afro-American man?
When we kill our brothers, rape our sisters, rob our families
Is this what it takes to be an Afro-American man?
We have the strength to be a REAL man
A wise man
A man your kids can look up to
A husband for your wife who takes care of her and does right
For every person can see
What it takes to be an Afro-American man
A real man
From slaves to some of the strongest and most important men in the world
Why Mr. Afro-American Man are we killing?
Full jail and funeral homes
Mr. Afro-American Man
Let's live together and love one another
Mr. Afro-American Man
Grow strong, believe in God, and let the world know
What it takes to be a REAL MAN "Mr. Afro-American Man"

~ Poetry of a Man's Soul ~

The Mind And Words Of A Child, is a poem about people and their hearts

The Mind And Words Of A Child

Why do people look at you and lie?
A child will ask you why
A child would say "Hey Mister, your breath don't smell good!"
And you would say nothing because you know its true
When you look at a friend's baby for the first time
You will say, "Oh, what a pretty baby."
Then a kid would say
"Man, that's the ugliest baby I have ever seen."
Sad but true and you know it too
You walk into a store with your kids and there's a man stealing
You know right from wrong and your kids do too
You told them that it was wrong to steal
Then your kids ask you why's that man stealing?
You would say, "It's not your business."
When are we going to be like a child with hearts so true?
Tell people the things that they do are so wrong to do
When you have an opinion, you just say nothing and walk away
It's time to have a mind and truthful words
It's time for people like you and me to stand tall
Tell the truth about things going wrong
Let the World know what's right and what's wrong
Just have the mind and words of a child.

~ Poetry of a Man's Soul ~

Where My Heart Is is a poem about AMERICA. What a great place to live. If we, the people, don't watch out, we all are going to lose her.

Where My Heart Is

Out of all the places in the world that I have been
I must say with all my heart America is the best
When I came home to AMERICA, land of the free
There's no place I'd rather be
I love America with all my heart
We the people must never part
People might hate me for my color
I just wish we all could live together in the Land of the Free
This is a land where all men can live free
White, Red, Yellow, and Black
We all need to live together
I never saw blacks going to AFRICA to live
Whites going back to ENGLAND
Yellow going back to ASIA
Or Red men back to MEXICO
It's people coming to AMERICA, the land of the free
It's time for us all to find out what we all were put here for
White, Red, Yellow, and Black
This is America
This is where my heart is
We have to live together
If not, we're all going to die together
In this land where all men can be free
Where all things can be yours, if you want it to be
So please... don't take my heart away from me

~ Poetry of a Man's Soul ~

What's The Matter With This World, is a poem about our WORLD. Everybody says that we have a problem with this WORLD. There's nothing the matter with this WORLD. The problem with this WORLD is THE PEOPLE

What's The Matter With This World

What's the matter with this WORLD
There's nothing the matter with this WORLD
The problem with this WORLD is the people
Some people don't understand right from wrong
They don't know what family stands for
They don't know the love for a human life
A Woman or a Man doesn't know who they are
When there's drugs, murder, rape and killing children
You will say what's the matter with this world?
People, this world doesn't have a problem
It's just you and me that are going crazy every day
It makes me sad to see our "so called" leaders on TV
They say they don't know what the problem is today
They're afraid if they say something out the way
They will lose a vote today
When are we, the real people, going to stand up today
And start believing back into this world today?

~ Poetry of a Man's Soul ~

My Child Was Born Today, is a poem about a man and his love for his child. This is about what every man should feel when his child is born into this world.

My Child Was Born Today

I looked at my child for the very first time today
When he looked back at me and started to cry
I said, "It's Dad my child.
I'm here to love you, to take care of you in every way."
I looked at my child knowing that he didn't ask to be here
But with God's help from up above and the love from me
With all my heart I am going to love thee
When things go wrong, Dad will be there for you
When you're sad, Dad hopes he can make things happy for you
When things in the world are so bad, Dad will be there
I'll teach you right from wrong
Most of all, Dad would like to say that
I'm always here besides you
I'll help you and love you in every way
Thank God for my child

~ Poetry of a Man's Soul ~

What Am I Going To Do This Summer, is a poem about the love that a child has for her mother and father and how divorce has taken away someone they love

What Am I Going To Do This Summer

This summer I am going to the beach
Then after that, I am going to be at Six Flags Over Georgia
Then I am going to my daddy's house to get my dog
My friend Dayka is coming to the beach
My mother is coming to the beach
She is going to sit in the car correctly
My dad is driving us to the beach and
I am making sure he doesn't fall asleep
I will not argue with my friend Dayka like we always do
We must try to get my mother and father back together today
So we can't play no kind of way
I told Dad to bring some flowers
I told Mother to bring the chicken that Dad loves
I don't care what it takes
I'm going to get my family back together again!

by Tiffany Arnold
June 8, 1988 (Second Grade)

~ Poetry of a Man's Soul ~

Hunger, is a poem about hunger in the U.S.A. This country should be a place where there's plenty of food for everyone. We, as a people, should stop hunger in the U.S.A.!

Hunger

When you think about hunger, you think about being in a desert
Where there is no water and food around
The only thing around you that you can see is sand
The sun is hot
How can you think about hunger in the USA
We look at TV and they say "Send money!"
So they can send it far away?
Why when we have American hunger every day
Is it a game that our government wants to play?
Let our kids, families, and friends go hungry every day?
Every Thanksgiving and Christmas, we feed the hungry
Are we doing it out of guilt because we ignored them the other days?
I know you will say, "So what. I work every day. So should they!"
What you said may be so right but there are no jobs or places to stay
Would you put up a homeless person or feed them today?
We all are on a fixed income that is living from day to day
Remember, it could be me or you hungry one say
In the USA, there should not be hunger every day
Why?
Because we, the people, must stop it in every way
Stop HUNGER IN THE U.S.A.

~ Poetry of a Man's Soul ~

Who Shall We Love, is a poem asking people if they should live the way God planned. If you let people change your mind because of peer pressure, you are not living your truth. Look inside yourself for the answer to what's right and what's wrong. If the answer is not good for all people and the future of all mankind, then look deeper into your heart and right way.

Who Shall We Love

What do I say?
Is it right or wrong for a MAN to love a MAN?
Or a WOMAN to love a WOMAN?
Should everybody do it or just a few?
Do they have the right like me and you?
Or, are they trying to tell me as a man to love a MAN?
Why do you think that others hate them so?
Is it because we don't understand they want to live that way?
Man has been loving man throughout time, but if we all do it
There won't be any future to live up to
Where would our future come from?
Who will have our kids?
If you believe in God, the BIBLE, or ADAM and EVE,
Not ADAM and STEVE or EVE and SUE
But whatever you do, it's up to YOU
Don't make me feel like I am the bad guy for the way you are
God gives each of us a mind. Is yours ok?
Whatever a man or a woman does, it's all up to them
What I'm saying is that it's ok for mankind to grow
And have a future for all to look up to
So do whatever makes you happy
Because I'm not God to tell you what to do
Who shall we love is up to you
But, is it right to do for the future to look to?

~ Poetry of a Man's Soul ~

American Cowboy Who Is He, is a poem encouraging all kids to be whatever they want to be. They should find out things about themselves instead of listening to someone telling them what they can't be. It's all up to you to be what you want to be.

AMERICAN COWBOY WHO IS HE

When I was a little boy I always wanted to be a cowboy
My dream was to have two guns, a pretty horse and to fight bad guys
One day when I was playing I asked my friends
Could I be a hero and the star?
They said there's no such thing as a black cowboy
With tears in my eyes, I ran home and started to cry
It was as if someone has taken my heart out of me
I ran to tell my father that I don't want these guns
I no longer wanted my Roy Roger pictures and he asked why
Because my friends said that there is no such thing as a black cowboy
Why can't I be a black cowboy if I wanted to be one?
With tear in his eyes, my father said, "This is America.
You can be what you want to be.
If you wanted to be a cowboy, that's what you're going to be."
He took me by the hand and read me a book about cowboys
In this book it said one out of every four cowboys was a black man
There was a sheriff, marshall, a black town, and some bad guys
But most of all, they were REAL COWBOYS
I went back to my room and got my two guns and my horse
AND I told them all...
"I am a REAL COWBOY!"

~ Poetry of a Man's Soul ~

Hate, is a poem about why we, as a people, must be so hateful when there is so much love in this world. Why should we take hate to our graves?

HATE

Why do you HATE?
Have you ever wondered why?
Was it something that was out into you?
Are you born with it?
Do you hate your neighbor that lives next door?
Have you ever stopped to think why?
Do you hate him for what he is or do you even know why?
To just look at a human and say that you hate him is so sad
People hate for all reasons. What's yours?
Does it make sense to just hate someone?
With all of the love in this world, why do people hate?
Don't hate a man because of the color of his skin
Don't hate him because of what he believes in
Don't hate a man because of his religion or what he stands for
There's so many ways to hate
Do you need it?
Look at yourself and ask is it worth it?
We have just a short time on this earth
With hate in your heart, how can you enjoy life?
So whatever someone does to you try to forgive them
And with all of your heart, try to love them

~ Poetry of a Man's Soul ~

Divorce, is a poem about people and marriage. 6 out of 10 couples will divorce and then marry again. What are we doing to our loved ones? We need to look within ourselves before we say I DO. Divorce is NOT a game to play with people's LIFE

DIVORCE

Divorce?
What does it do to you and me?
How can it be true that you want a divorce from me
After all we have been through, how can we get a divorce?
Was I so bad that you can't live with me?
Or was it something that you wanted to do?
How can you tell me that you hate me in less than five years?
You told me you loved me
How can you really hate me now?
How could our love be so true and today it's just a lie?
What shall I tell our kids?
MOTHER and FATHER don't love each other?
Some of our friends said that it wouldn't last
It would all come to an end
Where has our love gone?
Was it just something to do?
Why get married just to turn around and divorce?
How can we lose all the love we had?
Is it just a joke to you?
Is this the end for YOU and ME and OUR FAMILY?
Divorce?

~ Poetry of a Man's Soul ~

Why Am I So Lucky, is a poem about a man's love and the love his woman has for him. Out of all the women in this world, she belongs to me. There are some good women in the world and when you find one, thank GOD for her. You'll find yourself asking, "Why am I so lucky?"

WHY AM I SO LUCKY

Why am I so lucky to have someone like you?
Out of all the men in the world, it's me that you look up to
And out of all the men in the world, God gave me to you
When I look at you, I ask could it be true
How could you be in love with me?
You're so pretty and I'm just an average guy
Tell me why you are so in love with me
The little things that you do tell me you love me for me
The way you love me
My whole world is based around you
Until the day I die, I like to thank God for you
Most of all...I love you
I'm such a lucky guy!

~ Poetry of a Man's Soul ~

Why Do I Love You, is a poem about the way a man loves his woman and most of all WHY

WHY DO I LOVE YOU

I love you because of your lovely smile
I love you because of you lovely arms
That way you kiss me and hold me tight
I love you because of your lovely eyes
They shine so bright
I love you because of the way you tell me you love me so
Most of all, I love you because you are mine
I love you with all my heart

~ Poetry of a Man's Soul ~

To Be Ready To Go, is a poem about life and what it holds for you and me as we walk the street. Today are our hearts and souls ready to go?

TO BE READY

When you walk out your door every morning
Do you wonder if you will come back home?
Do you know what life holds for you when you walk out that door?
Do you know that every day you're in a war?
All you think about is finishing 8 hours a day at your job
What day is this?
Is it your day to go?
When you walk into the grocery store, do you care what day it is?
You might see your maker
Are you ready?
When you walk out that door
Do you tell your wife and kids how you love them so?
Do you thank your maker for this day?
We MUST be ready when we walk out that door
For no reason, a man with a gun might say it's time for you to go

~ Poetry of a Man's Soul ~

When You're Born Poor, is a poem about people that need someone to look up to and need a helping hand from you and me.

When You're Born Poor

When you're born poor, who do you turn to?
Who do you look up to?
When everything around you is so sad and blue
What's in your heart?
Where should a person turn to?
When you look around, all you know is the ground
When you never know where your next meal is coming from
Should you look for a handout from people that don't care
Later they only say the words you hate to hear
"You're poor....Get out of here!"
When you start to take things just to live
They will lock you up and call you a thief
When you try to get a job
They will look at you as though you're no good
Even where your children go to school
They pick at them and call them names
When you try to do better for yourself
They will say that you'll never be any good
So you start to drink to make things better
And when life is over, they all will say
What a poor person
Why did he have to live that way?

~ Poetry of a Man's Soul ~

Your 50th Birthday, is a poem is about the love a man has for his wife. He doesn't care about her age because he knows in his heart that he will always love her for the rest of his life.

Your 50th Birthday

Today they said you're having a birthday
When you turned 30, they said that you were getting better
When you turned 40, they said you were the best that you ever were
Now you're turning 50
What do they say?
As I look at you everyday, I see what I saw when you were 21
A pretty lady that I asked to be my wife
To love me until death do us part
So today when you turn 50, I would like to say
I need you
I love you
I want you in every way
Because today I see a lady that looks like she's 21
And in my heart I will always love you
So to you my dear, I love you and HAPPY BIRTHDAY
On your 50th Birthday

~ Poetry of a Man's Soul ~

Final Thoughts

POETRY OF A MAN'S SOUL is a book for all AMERICANS to read. As I sat down to write, I think about we as people, white, red, yellow and black. What do we fight for? Why are we killing one another? Why are there drugs, murder, rape, hate, hunger, and welfare? Why can't you tell me why things are so bad in the U.S.A.? We have so many colors. Are people dying to make America FREE? In 1776 AMERICA was set FREE. It allowed us to live as "We The People". In that address it said that all MEN were FREE. In 1864, they fought in a civil war. Today, what are we fighting for? I'd like to know. We work together. We go across the sea and die together. Why can't we live together? We shop in the same stores together. What is it about the color of a man's skin that makes some men hate? There are all kinds of hate groups that hate a man if he's not one color. It's not the time to hate one another. It's time to live together. Go love one another.

You have all kinds of groups from so-called Asian Americans, Cuban American, African American, and many more came to be FREE. But this is only one AMERICA. We need to stop dividing ourself into different groups because we live in the same AMERICA and we should only be AMERICANS...ONE PEOPLE!

They have an old saying in Florida "The last American brings the flag." Is that the way it should be? We keep on killing and hating one another. White against Black, Yellow against Red? Tell me is that the way of America?

There is hunger every day. We fight to feed the hungry around Thanksgiving and Christmas. It's as though they think people are only hungry that time of the year. Shouldn't we feel guilty for the whole year? So many have plenty. So many Americans have nothing to eat or a safe place to sleep at night. Why in AMERICA? It's the land of plenty. Why is there a need for welfare for people to live on? Wasn't it back in the 40's when they started this so-called welfare for people to live on. People need a future and not a handout.

Our government pays farmers not to farm or raise livestock with our tax dollars. This ensures that the price of food won't go down.

Do you know or do you care? We all are little monkeys in a barrel. And there are just a few that tell us what to do. You never get a raise on you job and everything becomes more expensive. If that's not bad, miss 2 pay checks and try to catch up on you bills. It's time to be AMERICAN again. What did our people fight for? This is not for just one color. It's for all of us to stand tall. Don't pay you taxes and they will take what little you own and put you in jail. Then, they will take your tax dollars everyday and spend it on whatever they want. Is this AMERICA LAND OF THE FREE? Who's running this country? Is it you and me or just a few?

Rich people don't care because they are the ones that are running the show. The poor don't care as long as there is WELFARE to live on. It's you and me in the middle that's got to get this wake up call. I guess you ask how can we do this without starting a war? It's just as obvious as the nose on your face. It's called VOTING. It's those GOOD OL' Boys that run the place. It's time for a new marshall in town every four years. We put the same people back into office that run our government. Why can's they be limited to only for years in office?

Tell me, tell me, I know we all aren't crazy. Why would a man spend millions of dollars for a job that only pays $400,000? Four years later, he turns around and spends it again? Why in the world would a man in his right mind, spend millions and millions to run for a job that pays less than what he spent? Are they taking the job for something else? It's time for a change! Get off your butts and VOTE for something

~ Poetry of a Man's Soul ~

new and take back AMERICA. Stop listening to people and listen to yourself. You know right from wrong. You have your own opinions. Don't vote for a person because he's you color. Vote for him because he believes in what you believe. If he is elected and they change their mind on your "idea", Thank God this is America. The next four years you run for a change. It's time to live in country with a strong truthful foundation. It's time to change things around.

Crime. WE, as a people, can put all kinds of laws on the books but if we don't fairly enforce them, we are losers. Our young children need help! Jail or prison is not what they need. Where do we start? This must start with a special word and that word is FAMILY.

We need more families that include a Mother and a Father. We need more love in us for the kids. We need less divorce and child abuse and all this wrong must come to a stop!

    We just need to take the time to try and love one another and see in our hears what the problem is. Our children's futures are in our hands. It's not too late to make a change for the BETTER!

Poetry Of A Man's Soul II

- Coming Soon!!!

www.ingramcontent.com/pod-product-compliance
Lightning Source LLC
Chambersburg PA
CBHW071021080526
44587CB00015B/2448